Barack Obama
FOR BEGINNERS®
AN ESSENTIAL GUIDE

Barack Obama
FOR BEGINNERS®
AN ESSENTIAL GUIDE

BY BOB NEER • ILLUSTRATED BY JOE LEE

FOR BEGINNERS®

an imprint of Steerforth Press
Hanover, New Hampshire

For Beginners LLC
62 East Starrs Plain Road
Danbury, CT 06810 USA
www.forbeginnersbooks.com

Text: © 2008 Bob Neer
Illustrations: © 2008 Joe Lee
Cover Photo: AP Photo/Jae C. Hong
Cover/Book Design: David Janik

*This book was prepared without the involvement of any political party
or campaign.*

A For Beginners® Documentary Comic Book
Copyright © 2008

Cataloging-in-Publication information is available from the Library of Congress.

ISBN# 978-1-934389-38-6

Manufactured in the United States of America

For Beginners® and Beginners Documentary Comic Books® are published
by For Beginners LLC.

First Edition

10 9 8 7 6 5 4 3 2 1

Table of Contents

Complete source notes and additional information about Barack Obama and For Beginners Books, including links to numerous relevant videos and a timeline of events in the life of Barack Obama, are available at BarackObamaForBeginners.com. Visit us online!

I. ORIGINS 1961-1985

Barack Obama is a blend of extraordinary diversity: parents from Kenya and Kansas; an education in Indonesia, Hawaii, California, New York, and Massachusetts; employment in Chicago's poorest communities, leading law firms, and premier university; elected positions in the Illinois and United States Senates; and best-selling books that merge personal history and political action.

The result is a politician who asserts that we are all linked, and that while idealism must serve realism, pragmatism requires purpose. His latest book, which carries the inspirational title *The Audacity of Hope*, contains the following conclusion: "We should be guided by what works."

The Obama family traces its modern lineage to Hussein Onyango Obama, a Kenyan member of the Luo tribe born in 1895 near Lake Victoria. Onyango was a restless man of ambition. He was one of the first in his village to wear western clothing, walked for two weeks to Nairobi to find work, braving leopards and other dangers, and served with the British armed forces in World War I. He visited Europe, Myanmar and Sri Lanka as a soldier and briefly converted to Christianity, but abandoned it for Islam and added "Hussein" to his name following the war.

Senator Obama's father, Barack Hussein Obama, Sr., was born in 1936 in Nyangoma-Kogelo, Siaya District, also near Lake Victoria, to Onyango's second wife Akumu. She quarreled with her husband and left when Barack was nine. The boy was raised by Onyango's third wife. He was a precocious student but chafed at traditional village employment, which included tending goats. He took success in high school for granted, became boastful and truculent, and was expelled. He quarreled with his father, left the family lands, married his first wife Kezia in 1954 at age 18, and by his early 20s found himself employed as a shop boy in Nairobi with two children and little money. A pair of American teachers befriended him and helped him apply to U.S. universities. In 1959 he secured admission, after many rejections, to the University of Hawaii to study economics: the institution's first African student.

Obama, Sr. wore religion lightly. "Although my father had been raised a Muslim, by the time he met my mother he was a confirmed atheist, thinking religion to be so much superstition," his son has written.

Obama's mother's family history begins with her parents Madelyn Payne and Stanley Dunham—grandparents of Barack Obama who cared for him during high school. Payne was a Kansan raised by "stern Methodist parents who did not believe in drinking, playing cards or dancing." Nonetheless, their daughter, one of the best students in her high school graduating class, often visited Wichita to listen to big bands. On one of these outings, she met Stanley Dunham from the oil-town of El Dorado, Kansas, a furniture salesman "who could charm the legs off a couch." Dunham was a Baptist from the "other side of the railroad tracks." It later emerged that he was also a seventh cousin, once removed, of Vice-President Dick Cheney and also a seventh cousin, twice removed, of President Harry S Truman. Payne's family did not approve of the liaison, and the pair married in secret a few weeks before Madelyn graduated from high school. She told her parents after she received her diploma.

During World War II, Dunham joined the Army and served under General George S. Patton. Madelyn worked on a Boeing B-29 assembly line in Wichita. Obama's mother, Stanley Ann Dunham, was born in 1942 at Fort Leavenworth, Kansas. But her father wanted a boy, thus the name, which grieved the girl.

Dunham moved the family frequently: California, Kansas, Texas, and finally Mercer Island in Washington state—now a high end home for wealthy Seattle residents, then a somewhat isolated and bucolic suburb. Madelyn became vice-president of a local bank. The family attended the East Shore Unitarian Church. Ann, as she preferred to be known, thrived in the intellectual atmosphere of the local high school, where her philosophy teacher challenged his classes with texts like *The Organization Man*, *The Hidden Persuaders*, and *1984*. She was offered admission to the University of Chicago in 1958 at the age of 16. Her father said she was too young to go.

In 1960, Ann graduated from high school and the family moved to Hawaii. Stanley got a job at a large furniture store, Madelyn at the Bank of Hawaii, and they bought a house near the University of Hawaii. Ann, 18, enrolled as a freshman. In a Russian language class, she met Barack Obama, Sr., 23, who told her he was divorced. They gathered with friends on weekends to listen to jazz and discuss politics and world affairs. Ann was the only woman. She was, "the original feminist," according to Neil Abercrombie, now a Democratic congressman from Hawaii who participated in the meetings.

On 2 February 1961 the pair slipped away to Maui and were married. The wedding—Obama, "black as pitch," Ann, "white as milk"—would have been illegal in 22 states. Ann dropped out of college. On 4 August Barack Hussein Obama Jr. was born at the Kapi' olani Medical Center in Honolulu. The motto of the hospital was *Kulia I Ka Nu'u:* "Strive for the Highest."

The couple moved into a small apartment near the university. The following year, just three years after he had arrived, Obama completed his studies. He obtained two offers of admission to obtain a Ph.D. in economics. The first, from Harvard, was unfunded. The second, from the New School in New York, included a stipend. Obama chose Harvard. Unfunded, he did not take his family. He left Ann and his son in Honolulu.

In 1963, Ann returned to college. Food stamps helped support the family. After two years, her husband still absent, she filed for divorce.

At the East-West Center at the university she met Lolo Soetoro, an Indonesian oil company manager. In 1967 he proposed, she graduated, and the three moved to his home on the outskirts of Jakarta. Barack Obama Jr., then six years old, was impressed by the change. Soetoro had acquired a pet monkey for him. Baby crocodiles inhabited the garden. He learned to speak Indonesian and attended the local Catholic Franciscus Assisi Primary School. "The children of farmers, servants and low-level bureaucrats had become my friends, and together we ran the streets morning and night, hustling odd jobs, catching crickets, battling swift kites with razor-sharp lines—the loser watching his kite soar off with the wind," he wrote later in his memoir.

The family prospered. Soetoro got a job in the government relations office of a U.S. oil firm. Ann was hired to teach English at the U.S. Embassy. They moved to the affluent Menteng neighborhood in Jakarta. Obama transferred to SDN Menteng 1, an elite secular public elementary school that served primarily middle- and upper-class children, including several grandchildren of President Suharto. He was the only foreigner.

For administrative purposes, Obama was registered as a Muslim at this school, as at the Catholic institution, because that was the religion of his stepfather. He learned about Islam for two hours each week. His mother did not belong to any denomination. Nonetheless, Obama wrote, "My mother was in many ways the most spiritually awakened person I have ever known. . . . She possessed an abiding sense of wonder, a reverence for life and its precious, transitory nature." When he was a child, she would wake him to see a spectacular moon, or tell him to close his eyes to listen to the rustle of leaves as they walked together at twilight. "But she had a healthy skepticism of religion as an institution. And as a consequence, so did I." His step-father enjoyed alcohol and was not devout. Obama has never been a practicing Muslim.

The harshness of life was never distant in Jakarta. Later, Obama remembered, "[T]he face of the man who had come to our door one day with a gaping hole where his nose should have been: the whistling sound he made as he asked my mother for food. . . . [and] the time that one of my friends told me in the middle of recess that his baby brother had died the night before of an evil spirit brought in by the wind."

His mother under-stood. "She had learned . . . the chasm that separated the life chances of an American from those of an Indonesian. She knew which side of the divide she wanted her child to be on. I was an American, she decided, and my true life lay elsewhere," Obama remembered.

The means she chose to achieve this end was education. The family did not have enough money for Obama to attend a private international school, so his mother subscribed to a series of elementary school correspondence courses. Each weekday, starting at 4:00 a.m., Dunham taught Obama his English lessons for three hours before he went to school and she left for work.

She also taught him values. "'If you want to grow into a human being,' she would say to me, 'you're going to need some values.' Honesty . . . Fairness . . . Straight talk . . . and independent judgment," Obama wrote. "In a land where fatalism remained a necessary tool for enduring hardship, where ultimate truths were kept separate from day-to-day realities, she was a lonely witness for secular humanism, a soldier for New Deal, Peace Corps, position-paper liberalism," he added.

His stepfather taught him how to fight, and about the nature of power. One afternoon he laced boxing gloves onto the boy's hands. "My hands dangled at my sides like bulbs at the ends of thin stalks. . . . He adjusted my elbows, then crouched into a stance and started to bob. 'You want to keep moving, but always stay low—don't give them a target. How does that feel?'" Obama wrote. Later he offered advice. "'The strong man takes the weak man's land. He makes the weak man work in his fields. If the weak man's woman is pretty, the strong man will take her.' He paused to take another sip of water, then asked, 'Which would you rather be?'. . . 'Better to be strong . . . If you can't be strong, be clever and make peace with someone who's strong. But always better to be strong yourself. Always.'"

Obama's half-sister, Auma Soetoro, was born in 1970.

By 1971, the correspondence courses were complete. His mother's father, who had abandoned the furniture business for insurance sales, enlisted the help of his boss, an alumnus, to gain admission for Obama to Punahou Academy, founded in 1841, the most prestigious private school in Hawaii. Current tuition for the school is $15,725. Obama won a scholarship. "My first experience with affirmative action, it seems, had little to do with race," Obama wrote later. He returned to Hawaii in the summer, moved back in with his grandparents, who now lived in a modest two bedroom apartment, and started fifth grade.

The new school was a shock: socially, culturally, and racially. Many of the other fifth graders had been together since kindergarten; Obama's Indonesian sandals were dowdy and his clothes out of style; and he was one of just two black children in the class.

His mother and sister joined him the following year. Ann had been admitted to a master's program to study the anthropology of Indonesia at the University of Hawaii. The family moved into a small apartment and lived on Ann's graduate student grants. Their circumstances were a sharp contrast to the affluence of some of Obama's classmates. Then suddenly, surprisingly, two weeks after Ann's return, Obama's father decided to visit. He had received an M.A. from Harvard, taken a job with a U.S. oil company, returned to Kenya, married a woman named Ruth Nidesand he met in Cambridge, and fathered two children with her. He served as an economist for the Kenyan Ministry of Transportation and a senior economist in the Kenyan Ministry of Finance before falling out with President Kenyatta, losing his position, and beginning a decline into poverty and drinking from which he never recovered. Obama Sr. had been in a car accident and decided to spend a month in Hawaii to recuperate. Obama's time with his father was brief, but poignant. "For brief spells in the day I will lie beside him, the two of us alone in the apartment sublet from a retired old woman whose name I forget . . . and I read my book while he reads his. He remains opaque to me . . . But I grow accustomed to his company," he wrote. "Two weeks later he was gone," Obama added. Forever.

The postscript to the story of Obama's father was a sad one. He was divorced from Ruth and experienced a period of destitution. He suffered another bad automobile accident. Both legs were amputated and he lost his job. He married for a fourth time, despite continued problems with alcohol, and had a son. He died in 1982 at age 46 in a final automobile accident. Obama learned of his death, a few months after his 21st birthday, in a brief telephone call from a relative in Kenya he had never met.

His mother, who had advanced to a Ph.D. program after completing her master's degree, completed her coursework and moved to Indonesia with Auma in 1975 to do field work for her dissertation. Obama, about to begin high school, chose to remain in Hawaii. He moved back in with his grandparents.

This was a time of searching. "I was trying to raise myself to be a black man in America, and beyond the given of my appearance, no one around me seemed to know exactly what that meant," Obama wrote. He looked for answers in books. He read the works of great black American intellectuals: James Baldwin, Ralph Ellison, Langston Hughes, Richard Wright, and W.E.B. DuBois. But each of these men wound up disappointed and withdrawn. Only Malcolm X's autobiography, his repeated acts of self-creation, Obama said, offered something different. But even that would not provide the answers Obama was seeking. He found himself "utterly alone."

He sought a release through drugs: marijuana, alcohol, and sometimes cocaine when he could afford it. "I got high ... [to] push questions of who I was out of my mind," he wrote.

Over time, he adopted two responses to race-based realities in the culture around him. At the broadest level, he accepted, did not blame, and hoped for change. He told an African-American friend who urged him to push for more basketball playing time, for example, that the other players, "play like white boys do, and that's the style coach likes us to play, and they're winning the way they play. I don't play that way."

He could see the possibility of a better society, however—he longed for it—and began to think about how he and others might work proactively to bring about change. What he sought to avoid was "withdrawal into a smaller and smaller coil of rage, until being black meant only the knowledge of your own powerlessness, of your own defeat." As a practical matter, he wrote, "People were satisfied so long as you were courteous and didn't make any sudden moves."

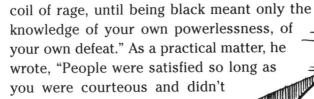

An important early decision Obama made was where to go to college. It is possible in retrospect to see his choice of Occidental College in Los Angeles as a first step toward broader opportunities on the mainland. That is not how Obama saw it. He had met a girl from Brentwood, a tony suburb of the city, on vacation in Hawaii and wanted to be closer to her. So he chose Occidental, which also offered a full scholarship, from among the several schools to which he had been admitted. He enrolled in 1979.

He spent his first years in college having a good time. He studied, but not too seriously. He dabbled in politics, including some work on the campus campaign to urge Occidental to divest from South Africa, but not too deeply. He started down the same road of withdrawal and anger he had traveled in Honolulu. Then after a long night of smoking, drinking, and listening to Billie Holiday, he considered challenges thrown at him by some of his peers at the college, and had an epiphany. "I rose from my couch and opened my front door, the pent-up smoke trailing me out of the room like a spirit. . . . Who told you that being honest was a white thing? they asked me. Who sold you this bill of goods, that your situation exempted you from being thoughtful or diligent or kind, or that morality had a color? You've lost your way, brother. Your ideas about yourself—about who you are and who you might become—have grown stunted and narrow and small." Years later, Senator Obama had this to say about his early, angry incarnation: "You know, what puzzles me is why people are puzzled by that. That angry character lasts from the time I was fifteen to the time I was twenty-one or so. I guess my explanation is I was an adolescent male with a lot of hormones and an admittedly complicated upbringing. But that wasn't my natural temperament."

A second important decision, to transfer to Columbia College in 1981 through a program arranged between the two schools, was more purposeful. Harlem offered a larger black community; Columbia the diversity of a great university; New York the eclecticism of the country's largest city. Obama wanted all of this.

His introduction to the city, however, was rough: a friend he planned to stay with on his first night never came home, and he spent the night propped up on his luggage in a vacant lot next door.

While he moved on, his mother's second marriage crumbled: she divorced his stepfather in 1980.

As his father had done at a similar age Obama, perhaps aware that the chips were down, now threw himself into his studies. He participated little in campus activities but devoted himself to philosophy and the intricacies of the university's offerings in political science and international relations. He wrote his senior thesis on Soviet nuclear disarmament.

At this point, he decided to try to become a community organizer, to help bring about change in black communities through grass roots efforts. He saw the task as a continuation of the work begun by the civil rights movement: "At night, lying in bed, I would let the slogans drift away, to be replaced with a series of images, romantic images, of a past I had never known. They were of the civil rights movement . . . the same images that my mother had offered me as a child. A pair of college students, hair short, backs straight, placing their orders at a lunch counter teetering on the edge of riot. . . . A county jail bursting with children, their hands clasped together, singing freedom songs." But, he said, he couldn't get an organizing job.

Instead, after he received his B.A. from Columbia in 1983, he took a job as a research assistant at Business International, a publishing and advisory firm with about 250 employees worldwide that helped U.S. companies operate overseas. He was soon promoted to the position of financial writer for a reference service called Financing Foreign Operations, and wrote for a newsletter called the *Business International Money Report.* "Forget about this organizing business and do something that's gonna make you some money," advised Ike, the gruff black security guard at his office building.

The pull of his dreams, however, proved too strong. In 1984, Obama resigned. He began to look again for the job he had dreamed of as a student. He turned down a conference organizing job with a prestigious civil rights organization because, he said, it was too far from the street. He worked for three months at City College in Harlem as an organizer for the New York Public Interest Research Group, an organization founded by Ralph Nader, at a salary of slightly less than $10,000 per year. Obama said he spent the time, "trying to convince minority students at City College about the importance of recycling." Former colleagues say the primary focus of activities was, "mass transit, higher education, tuition and financial aid issues." He spent a week handing out leaflets for the campaign of a Brooklyn assemblyman. The candidate lost and the campaign stiffed him on his salary. "In six months I was broke, unemployed, eating soup from a can," Obama remembered.

The walls were closing in. He had all but given up. Then, on a visit to the New York Public Library, browsing what he described as a "newsletter for do-gooder jobs," he spotted a help-wanted ad from the Developing Communities Project, a coalition of eight Catholic parishes on the South Side of Chicago, all with black congregations led by white priests. He called. Gerald Kellman, a Jewish convert to Catholicism, called back. He needed an organizer— a black organizer: the South Side is the largest African-American community in the country. The salary was $10,000 per year plus a $2,000 travel allowance to buy a car. It would go up if Obama made progress. He was off.

II. ASCENT 1985-96

Obama arrived in Chicago in June 1985: 23 years old, with a world to conquer. What he found was a physical and spiritual home.

His first assignment was to learn about the South Side. Kellman sent him to interview residents of Roseland—97.8% African-American: a community cut off from the city to the north by two freeways. For the next three weeks, and in a larger sense throughout his years as an organizer, Obama learned the past and present of some of the most disadvantaged people in the country.

His goal was to find issues around which to mobilize: paths to power. In this Kellman and Obama followed precepts laid down by the early Chicago activist Saul Alinsky. "Power comes in two forms—money and people. You haven't got any money, but you do have people," he had advised would-be reformers.

The formula for Obama was less prosaic. "Once I found an issue enough people cared about, I could take them into action. With enough actions, I could start to build power," he wrote.

There was a glimmer here of larger hopes. "The only answer is to build up local power bases that can merge into a national power movement that will ultimately realize your goals," Alinsky averred.

Obama's first major accomplishment, however, came from the top down. He glanced at the back of a brochure from the

Mayor's Office of Employment and Training (MET) and noticed the agency had no offices in the southernmost part of the city. He mobilized residents of the Altgeld Gardens housing project— squeezed between a landfill and a redolent sewage treatment plant at the city's southern edge; median 2000 household income $11,066; also 97% African-American—and pushed for a jobs center.

City Hall was receptive. Harold Washington, the first African-American mayor of Chicago, had been elected in April. Obama organized a public meeting with the director of the MET. He worked his team to exhaustion to ensure a tightly scripted event and a generous turnout. The tenant representatives pushed, and secured a promise for an intake center in six months. "The crowd broke into hearty applause," he remembered. Washington himself opened the office.

His second big effort was more dramatic, but ultimately less satisfying. According to Obama, an Altgeld tenant noticed that the Chicago Housing Authority was soliciting bids for removal of asbestos from the project's Management Office. According to Kellman, Obama spotted the bid notice. Either way, the Authority stonewalled tenant demands for an inspection of apartments for asbestos. Obama mobilized a busload of residents and descended on the offices of the executive director. With a few judiciously placed press invitations, the expedition yielded publicity and results. The authority agreed to test every unit. When asbestos was confirmed, stop-gap cleanup measures were instituted. "I changed as a result of that bus trip, in a fundamental way," Obama wrote later.

Over the long term, however, little happened to the asbestos in Altgeld. The CHA asked the department of Housing and Urban Development for over a billion dollars to repair housing projects across the city. The federal agency, which answered to President Reagan, offered money to repair plumbing and roofing problems, or remove asbestos, but not both. The problem remained unresolved during Obama's time as an organizer.

The lesson was plain. Significant change was possible with government support, and impossible without it.

Obama decided that law school would give him tools he needed to do more. Washington, after all, had graduated from the Northwestern University School of Law, and had "parlayed that lofty degree and his own personal charisma into a highly successful political career," in the words of *Chicago Tribune* reporter and Obama biographer David Mendell. "Washington could do more for Chicago's poor blacks with the wave of his veto pen than Obama could in countless days and nights of community meetings in Roseland and Altgeld," Mendell wrote.

He was accepted by Harvard. "I would learn power's currency, in all its intricacy and detail, knowledge that would have compromised me before coming to Chicago but that I could now bring back to where it was needed, back to Roseland, back to Altgeld; bring it back like Promethean fire," he wrote.

On the home front, Obama's existence in Chicago was as austere as in New York. "When I wasn't working, the weekends would usually find me alone in an empty apartment, making do with the company of books," he remembered. A girlfriend who lived with him for a time during this period, and his cat Max, evidently made little impression.

The organizer found spiritual solace, however, at the Trinity United Church of Christ, a South Side megachurch: in the community of its predominantly black congregation, and in the sermons of its minister Jeremiah Wright. Trinity—"Unashamedly Black and Unapologetically Christian" its motto—was the largest church affiliated with the United Church of Christ, a primarily white Protestant Christian denomination with roots in

Congregationalism, which branched from Anglo-American Puritanism. Wright, a former marine with degrees from Howard University and the University of Chicago Divinity School, built the church from 87 members in 1972 to over 8,500 by the 1980s. The congregation included people of all races and more than a few celebrities, including television host Oprah Winfrey.

A meeting with Wright, and more generally a "church home," was suggested to Obama as politically expedient by a minister he calls Reverend Philips in his autobiography: "It might help your mission if you had a church home, though. It doesn't matter where, really." He had faith in himself, Obama reflected, but, "Faith in one's self was never enough." He arranged a meeting with Wright.

The Reverend, as Obama describes him, was acutely aware of the challenges faced by African-Americans. "Life's not safe for a black man in this country, Barack. Never has been. Probably never will be," Obama recalled. The church he built, however, preached inclusion—and there Obama saw power. "By widening its doors to allow all who would enter, a church like Trinity assured its members that their fates remained inseparably bound, that an intelligible 'us' still remained. It was a powerful program, this cultural community, one more pliant than simple nationalism, more sustaining than my own brand of organizing," he concluded.

He woke before dawn on the day of his first visit for services, brushed the lint from his only suit, and arrived by 7:30 a.m. The title of the sermon was, "The Audacity to Hope," a phrase Obama later adapted for the title of his second book *The Audacity of Hope.* "White folks' greed runs a world in need, apartheid in one hemisphere, apathy in another hemisphere . . . That's the world!" Wright preached. But hope, the minister said, could cure those ills, bring us together, and light the way to a future of empathy, inclusiveness, and common purpose. "The audacity of hope! I still remember my grandmother, singing in the house, 'There's a bright side somewhere . . . don't rest until you find it,'" he said.

Obama let his imagination run, and his spirit soared. "At the foot of that cross, inside the thousands of churches across the city, I imagined the stories of ordinary black people merging with the stories of David and Goliath," he wrote later. "The blood that had spilled was our blood, the tears our tears; until this black church, on this bright day, seemed once more a vessel carrying the story of a people into future generations and into a larger world." A child sitting next to him offered him a tissue. He thanked the boy, and felt tears running down his cheeks. Later, despite some continued uncertainty, Obama wrote that he, "submitted myself to His will, and dedicated myself to discovering His truth," and joined the church.

The organizer began at Harvard Law School in the autumn of 1988. As at Columbia, he threw himself into his studies. He excelled, was elected to the Law Review as one of the approximately 40 top students in his class of about 550, and earned a golden ticket: a lavishly paid job as a summer associate at Sidley & Austin in Chicago.

The 120 year old firm was one of the largest in the country. It was a sign of Obama's appeal that he secured the job after his first year: summer positions, in effect months-long recruiting presentations, were normally reserved for second-year students closer to graduation. Sidley was located in an office tower at the heart of downtown: a metaphor for its place at the center of a network of personal contacts as broad as global business and as local as City Hall. He was in the entry hall of the establishment.

The most lasting connection Obama made at Sidley, however, was to his mentor: a young lawyer named Michelle Robinson, assigned to introduce him to the business. Robinson, one of just 14 African-American attorneys among hundreds of lawyers at the firm, was from the South Side. Her father was a city water plant employee, her mother a secretary. Michelle had graduated *cum laude* from Princeton in 1985 with a degree in Sociology, and from Harvard Law in 1988.

More important for Obama, she was charming and attractive. He asked her out. She demurred. He persisted. Finally, she agreed to attend a community-organizing session in a church basement. He delivered a passionate speech, she later recalled, about "the world as it is, and the world as it should be," in his words. On their first big date that summer they went to the Chicago Art Institute, strolled down Michigan Avenue and watched Spike Lee's *Do the Right Thing,* a gripping film about racial and ethnic conflict.

On 5 February 1990, Obama was elected the first African-American President of the Law Review. The journal was split between liberal and conservative factions. Obama positioned himself as a centrist, survived a series of run-off elections that reduced the initial field of 18 candidates, and won when the last conservative was voted out and that group swung its support to him. The event was national news and won him, at 28, a contract for his memoirs. He graduated in 1991.

Obama forsook the corporate world and judicial clerkships that are common destinations for Harvard Law Review Presidents and plunged back into Chicago organizing after school. His first job was director of Project Vote!, a registration program inspired by the massive effort that helped elect Washington in 1983. The group had a staff of 10 and attracted 700 volunteers. Driven by its slogan, "It's a Power Thing," the project added more than 150,000 primarily African-American voters, of a possible pool estimated at 400,000, to the rolls. For the first time in the city's history registrations in the 19 predominantly African-American wards outnumbered those in the 19 predominantly white wards. The message, according to Obama: "If the politicians in place now at city and state levels respond to African-American voters' needs, we'll gladly work with and support them. If they don't, we'll work to replace them."

Meanwhile, Michelle had left the law firm and, perhaps influenced by her boyfriend, become an assistant to Mayor Daley. She was, she later said, ready to get serious with Obama. He responded with philosophical musings about the value of the institution of marriage. An exchange on these lines sparked a diatribe from her at the end of an elegant restaurant dinner one night in 1991. Dessert arrived, with a box on the plate. Inside, a ring. "He said, 'That kind of shuts you up, doesn't it?'" she recounted later. The couple were married by Wright the following October.

In September 1992 Obama joined the faculty of the University of Chicago Law School as a lecturer, an adjunct position not eligible for tenure. He taught the basics of constitutional jurisprudence—the history, mechanics and implementation of the Constitution—to a seminar of 20-30 students. A world away, Obama's mother at last completed her almost 1,000 page Ph.D. dissertation on peasant blacksmithing in Indonesia and received her degree. She continued a career she had developed as a global authority on micro-finance lending in developing countries.

In February 1993, Obama accepted a position at the 12-attorney activist law firm of Davis, Miner, Barnhill & Galland. He spent most of his time representing community organizers, and pursuing discrimination claims and voting rights cases. The balance of his time was spent preparing legal briefs, contracts, and other documents. Notable case work included a lawsuit by the Association of Community Organizations for

Reform Now (ACORN) to force the state to implement its Motor Voter Act, and a suit that forced Chicago to redraw some ward boundaries. Perhaps most important, partner Judson Miner, who was Corporation Counsel in Washington's administration until the Mayor died of a sudden heart attack, introduced Obama to his circle of political acquaintants.

The Obamas rose steadily in the Chicago establishment. In 1992, he became a founding board member of Public Allies, a non-profit that sought to place young leaders in community organizing positions. In 1993, he joined the nine-member board of the Woods Fund, an early supporter of his Developing Communities Project. The next year, he joined the Joyce Foundation's board, another Chicago philanthropy. Michelle became Executive Director of the Chicago office of Public Allies in 1993, after her husband resigned from the board. Throughout this period, during his spare time—generally hours when most people sleep, especially those with two jobs—Obama wrote his memoir, *Dreams from My Father*, which was published in 1995.

In 1994 the congressman for the Illinois 2nd congressional district was indicted for a sexual relationship with an underage campaign volunteer, and resigned. A special election was called for November 1995. Alice Palmer, the state senator who represented Obama's district, decided to run. She knew Obama, and his interest in politics, from his organizing and community activity, work on Project Vote!, and association with Davis, Miner, among other activities. She told him she was willing to support him as her successor. He asked for a commitment that she would not enter the race, even if she lost her bid for Congress. She agreed. In July, at age 33, he launched his first campaign for public office.

Obama's mother was diagnosed with ovarian and uterine cancer the same year. She died in Hawaii on 7 November, aged 52. Her son, immersed in his campaign, was thousands of miles away. He terms this absence the greatest mistake of his life. Stricken, he traveled to Hawaii to help scatter her ashes in the

Pacific. "She was the kindest, most generous spirit I have ever known," he wrote in the preface to the 2004 edition of his memoir: "What is best in me I owe to her."

The honeymoon between Alice Palmer and Obama was short. She lost the 1995 special election, changed her mind, and decided to contest her Illinois Senate seat. Her supporters asked Obama to withdraw. He refused. Working quickly, Palmer gathered 1,580 nominating signatures, more than twice the required 757, and filed for the March primary just before the December deadline.

Obama called for unity, pragmatism, and a new approach to politics in his campaign. "Any solution to our unemployment catastrophe must arise from us working creatively within a multicultural, interdependent, and international economy," he told the *Chicago Reader* newspaper. "What if a politician were to see his job as that of an organizer, as part teacher and part advocate, one who does not sell voters short but who educates them about the real choices before them?" he mused. What he practiced, however, was more traditional politics. On the first working day of 1996 Obama's staff, including crack Chicago election law attorney Thomas Johnson, hired specially for the job, started a series of hearings at the Chicago Board of Election Commissioners to challenge the validity of Palmer's nominations, and those of his three other rivals. To those who complained that a voter registration activist and civil rights attorney should not use administrative procedures to limit ballot access, Obama replied that the issue was one of competence: "My conclusion was that if you couldn't run a successful petition drive, then that raised questions in terms of how effective a representative you were going to be." All of his opponents were disqualified and Obama ran unopposed in the March primary. He cruised to victory in the overwhelmingly Democratic district in the general election, and took his seat in the 59-member Senate in 1997 for a two-year term.

Democrats were in the minority in the Senate, which limited Obama's ability to advance legislation. His supporters did what they could to help. U.S. Senator Paul Simon and Abner Mikva, a former state legislator and Congressional representative from Obama's district, and also a one-time federal judge, recommended him to Emil Jones, the leader of Democratic forces in the Senate. Jones, a former city sewer inspector from the far South Side, came to view Obama as a son. Obama has called him his "political godfather."

Obama's greatest triumph in his first term was a new ethics and campaign finance bill that prohibited lawmakers from soliciting campaign funds on state property or accepting gifts from parties with interests in pending legislation. Jones let his friend manage the bill, which passed 52-4 in May 1998. In all, Obama introduced or was chief co-sponsor on 56 bills in his first two years, of which 14 became law. His successes included legislation that increased penalties for criminals who used so-called date rape drugs, improved efficiencies for municipal adjudication procedures, tightened sanctions on felons involved in gun running, and provided compensation to crime victims for some property losses.

On 4 July, Obama became a father when Michelle delivered Malia Ann. That autumn, he was promoted to Senior Lecturer at the University of Chicago Law School. He was responsible for three courses per year, and "regarded as a professor," in the words of the school. In November, he was overwhelmingly re-elected to the Senate for a four-year term.

The first year of his second term was his most successful yet. Obama co-sponsored almost 60 bills, of which 11 became law, almost one each month. The measures focused on health care and child welfare: increased funding for after-school programs, tightened scrutiny of nursing homes, and improved training in the use of heart defibrillators are three examples. With Democrats in the minority, Obama's bills required Republican support for passage; many garnered substantial bipartisan majorities.

Obama, however, was ambitious and sought higher office. He may at one time have aspired to follow Harold Washington as Mayor. By 1999, however, Richard M. Daley, the son of longtime Mayor Richard J. Daley, had been mayor for a decade. He was as secure in his position as the pope, and proved it in the February election by trouncing his challenger Congressman Bobby Rush, who represented Obama's district.

The Rush campaign had been an incompetent botch. The candidate's car was towed in the middle of a news conference to criticize the city's snow-removal efforts; when the press discovered he had $750 in unpaid parking tickets, he blamed his wife. Obama thought the former alderman, co-founder of the Illinois chapter of the Black Panther Party in 1968 and an incumbent since 1993, was vulnerable. He suspended his law practice, one of his three jobs at the time, and announced his candidacy for the U.S. Congress in September 1999.

BOBBY RUSH

Obama's effort suffered setbacks from the start. In October, Rush's son was shot, lingered for four days, and then died. The death prompted a wave of sympathy and forced Obama to stop campaigning for a time. He was attacked as inauthentic— a powerful charge in the heavily African-American district.

"Barack is viewed in part to be the white man in blackface in our community," said state Senator Donne Trotter, another candidate in the race. In December, in the week between Christmas and New Year's, the Senate unexpectedly scheduled a vote on a closely contested and important piece of gun control legislation. Obama, a supporter of the bill, was on an annual family trip to see his grandmother in Hawaii. His daughter became sick and could not travel. He missed the vote, which failed by three. "Sen. Barack Obama (D-Chicago), who has—had?—aspirations to be a member of Congress, chose a trip to Hawaii over public safety in Illinois," editorialized the *Chicago Tribune.*

The candidate campaigned frenetically. "We called him the Kenyan Kennedy," said a field worker, because he appeared on elevated subway platforms in the dead of winter without an overcoat, hat or gloves. He ultimately won the endorsement of the *Tribune,* but it was not enough. He lost 2-1 in the March, 2000 primary. Later, during redistricting after the 2000 census, Rush saw to it that Obama's street was cut out of his congressional district.

Obama's political capital was at a low ebb. So were his personal fortunes: his bank account was empty. The 2000 Democratic Convention was in Los Angeles. Obama managed a cheap air ticket. When he tried to rent a car, however, his card was rejected, and when he finally made it to the convention hall, he wasn't able to get a floor pass. He left disheartened. Then came the 9/11 attacks. After that, "The notion that somebody named Barack Obama could win anything—it just seemed pretty thin," he later remembered. The birth of his second daughter Natasha, nicknamed Sasha, on 7 June must have provided solace.

Hope returned, however, by the summer of 2002. He rejected the idea of a run for Attorney General or another state office, and decided to aim for the U.S. Senate. The incumbent, Republican Peter Fitzgerald, was going to retire: the field was open.

PENNY PRITZKER

Big races require big money. A friend lined up a meeting with Penny Pritzker, one of the leaders of a Chicago family with a fortune estimated at around $20 billion, including control of Hyatt Hotels. Late in the summer Obama loaded his wife and their daughters into their car and drove 45 minutes to Pritzker's lakefront summer home. They met. Pritzker approved. Doors to the establishment began to open.

With Pritzker on his side, Obama had the possibility—although not yet the reality—of money. His next step was to hire a consultant to craft his message and manage his "media"—free press coverage, and paid advertising. David Axelrod—a transplanted New Yorker, graduate of the University of Chicago, former *Tribune* reporter, and communications director for Paul Simon's 1984 U.S. Senate campaign—won the job for his business AKP Message & Media. He was impressed by Obama, and accepted an unusually small retainer.

Then Obama took a bold step. On 2 October, before a few hundred demonstrators gathered at Federal Plaza in downtown Chicago, he spoke out unequivocally against the invasion of

Iraq. "I don't oppose all wars," Obama said, "What I am opposed to is a dumb war. What I am opposed to is a rash war. . . . What I am opposed to is the attempt by political hacks like Karl Rove to distract us from a rise in the uninsured, a rise in the poverty rate, a drop in the median income." It was a hard speech to give, he said later to reporter Mendell: "I was about to announce for the United States Senate and the politics were hard to read then. Bush is at sixty-five percent [approval]. You didn't know whether this thing was gonna play out like the first Gulf War, and you know, suddenly everybody's coming back to cheering." Perhaps as a result, he said, "That's the speech I am most proud of."

DAVID AXELROD

In November Illinois Democrats, after a decade in the minority, regained control of the state Senate. Emil Jones became President. "You know, you have a lot of power," Obama later recalled he told Jones: "You can make the next U.S. senator." Jones, he said, replied, "Wow, that sounds good! Got anybody in mind?" Obama answered: "Yes—me." Jones did just that. He appointed Obama Chair of the Health and Human Services Committee and sent important bills his way. By the end of 2004, Obama had sponsored over 800 pieces of legislation. His accomplishments, in addition to his ethics reforms, included a bill that required police to audio- or videotape homicide interrogations, which was passed unanimously by the Senate, leadership of legislation to outlaw racial profiling, and death penalty reform.

In January 2004, with a framework for his fundraising and political operations in place, and a solid legislative track record, Obama announced his candidacy for U.S. Senate.

The state legislator polled third behind two main opponents among eight declared Democratic candidates. Blair Hull was a professional blackjack player who invested his winnings in a securities trading business he later sold for $531 million. He was believed to be the richest person ever to seek office in Illinois. Dan Hynes, the state comptroller, came from a politically connected family. His father Thomas had been the Cook County assessor—a powerful position in Chicago—and President of the Illinois Senate.

Hull announced he would spend $40 million to win the race. He hired a large team of top consultants, acquired a giant campaign bus, and plastered the state with advertisements. In short order, he was the front-runner.

But he had an Achilles heel. He had been married and divorced twice from his second wife. The papers for the second separation were sealed. Local media outlets sued to have them released on the grounds that Hull's candidacy warranted an exceptional level of public scrutiny. When it appeared likely, a few weeks before the election, that a judge would agree, Hull and his former wife Brenda Sexton released the records. They were explosive. On one instance, Sexton claimed, Hull, "hung on the canopy bar of my bed, leered at me and stated, 'Do you want to die?

I am going to kill you . . ."'" He had been arrested for allegedly hitting her, although authorities declined to press charges. Hull persevered in the race, but his support evaporated.

Obama then made short work of Hynes. His campaign theme, "Yes, we can," devised by Axelrod, caught the imagination of the electorate. His television advertisements galvanized support in the African-American community, and ultimately yielded 95 percent of their votes. In March 2004, he won the Democratic primary with 53 percent of the ballots compared to 24 percent for Hynes and about 10 percent for Hull.

Success had its price. Obama seemed diffident as victory appeared to draw close. Supporter Valerie Jarrett asked why he seemed down. "When he lifted his head to answer, a tear rolled down his cheek. 'I'm really going to miss those little girls,' he said," she recalled.

The Republican nominee in the general election was Jack Ryan, a handsome former investment banker worth as much as $96 million who also was willing to spend huge sums to win.

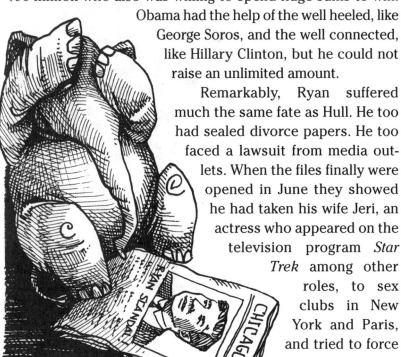

Obama had the help of the well heeled, like George Soros, and the well connected, like Hillary Clinton, but he could not raise an unlimited amount.

Remarkably, Ryan suffered much the same fate as Hull. He too had sealed divorce papers. He too faced a lawsuit from media outlets. When the files finally were opened in June they showed he had taken his wife Jeri, an actress who appeared on the television program *Star Trek* among other roles, to sex clubs in New York and Paris, and tried to force her to have sex with him in front of strangers. Ryan withdrew from the race three days later, leaving Obama without a Republican opponent.

A new star twinkled in the political firmament of the Democratic Party. Soon, Obama would shine even brighter. John Kerry, the Democratic nominee for president, asked him, still just a state senator, to deliver the keynote address at the Democratic National Convention in Boston. The slot carried live nationwide prime time television coverage and the attention of the world's media.

Obama titled the speech, "The Audacity of Hope," inspired by Reverend Wright's sermon. He began with his own story. "Let's face it, my presence on this stage is pretty unlikely," he said. He applauded American exceptionalism: "In no other country on Earth is my story even possible," he continued. We share common values, he asserted. "This year, in this election, we are called to reaffirm our values and our commitments, to hold them against a hard reality and see how we are measuring up to the legacy of our forbearers and the promise of future generations." The country, he maintained, had not met that measure. "And fellow Americans, Democrats, Republicans, independents, I say to you, tonight, we have more work to do . . ."

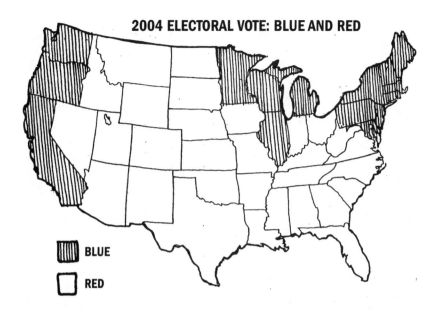

2004 ELECTORAL VOTE: BLUE AND RED

BLUE

RED

The only way to solve our problems, Obama argued, is together: "It is that fundamental belief—I am my brother's keeper, I am my sister's keeper—that makes this country work." He expanded on that idea in the heart of his address: "Now even as we speak, there are those who are preparing to divide us, the spin masters and negative ad peddlers who embrace the politics of anything goes. Well, I say to them tonight, there's not a liberal America and a conservative America; there's the United States of America. There's not a black America and white America and Latino America and Asian America; there's the United States of America. The pundits, the pundits like to slice and dice our country into red states and blue States: red states for Republicans, blue States for Democrats. But I've got news for them, too. We worship an awesome God in the blue states, and we don't like federal agents poking around our libraries in the red states. We coach little league in the blue states and, yes, we've got some gay friends in the red states. There are patriots who opposed the war in Iraq, and there are patriots who supported the war in Iraq. We are one people, all of us pledging allegiance to the stars and stripes, all of us defending the United States of America."

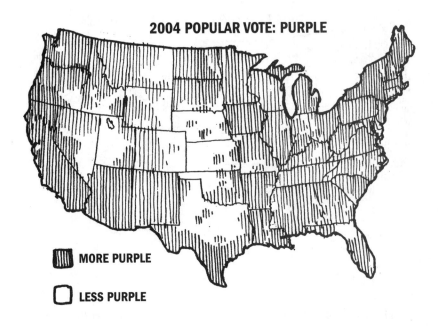

2004 POPULAR VOTE: PURPLE

▥ MORE PURPLE

◻ LESS PURPLE

Finally, he concluded, we must have hope: "Hope in the face of difficulty, hope in the face of uncertainty, the audacity of hope: In the end, that is God's greatest gift to us, the bedrock of this nation, a belief in things not seen, a belief that there are better days ahead." Reaction was overwhelmingly positive. Obama became famous.

The beleaguered Illinois Republican Party threw Maryland resident and two-time losing G.O.P. Presidential candidate Alan Keyes into the race in August. The former U.S. ambassador to the U.N. Economic and Social Conference under President Reagan had never lived in Illinois and never won an election. Obama beat him 70%-29%, the largest margin of victory ever in an Illinois Senate contest, and became the fifth African-American elected to the U.S. Senate. He resigned from the Illinois Senate and

ALAN
KEYES

the University of Chicago, and was sworn in to the U.S. Senate by Vice President Dick Cheney, his distant relative, on 4 January 2005.

The wind was at Obama's back. In October 2006 his second book, *The Audacity of Hope*, written in his spare time during his first year in the Senate, was released. It rose to the top of the *New York Times* bestseller list. Works by potential 2008 Democratic presidential candidates Hillary Clinton and John

Edwards languished far down on the list. Enormous enthusiastic crowds gathered for book signings at venues across the country. They attracted reporters who filed stories that further built attention. His advisors urged him to run for President. "He's ready, why wait? Obama in '08" read a popular Washington D.C. bumper sticker.

He consulted with Michelle. She said if he stopped smoking—a habit he had struggled with for years—she would support a bid. He quit.

On 11 February 2007, Obama stood in front of a crowd of 15,000 at the Illinois state capital, and announced his candidacy for president. "In the face of war, you believe there can be peace. In the face of despair, you believe there can be hope. In the face of a politics that's shut you out, that's told you to settle, that's divided us for too long, you believe we can be one people, reaching for what's possible, building that more perfect union," he said. "Each and every time, a new generation has risen up and done what's needed to be done. Today we are called once more—and it is time for our generation to answer that call. Together, starting today, let us finish the work that needs to be done, and usher in a new birth of freedom on this Earth." The race was on.

IV. CAMPAIGN FOR PRESIDENT

Obama built his run for president on relatively centrist positions, opposition to the war in Iraq, and a campaign operation that integrated community organizing techniques with the power of the Internet. He attended to both policy and practice on the day he announced his candidacy: first, he released a 63-page "Blueprint for Change," which described his platform; second, he launched a set of organizing tools at BarackObama.com. The result was a campaign whose message was delivered from the top down, but whose activism grew from the bottom up. Fundraising was everyone's job. Key elements of his successful U.S. Senate drive—the themes of unity and change, "Yes We Can" slogan, and top operatives—formed the core of his national effort.

Pragmatism was his policy touchstone. "We will do collectively, through our government, only those things that we cannot do as well or at all individually and privately," he wrote, quoting Lincoln.

Opportunity was the focus of his economic plan. Upward mobility, "has been at the heart of this country's promise since its founding," he wrote. "The resources and power of the national government can facilitate, rather than supplant, a vibrant free market," he added. He called for a middle class tax cut, an increase in the minimum wage, and a repeal of the Bush administration's tax breaks for households that earn more than $250,000.

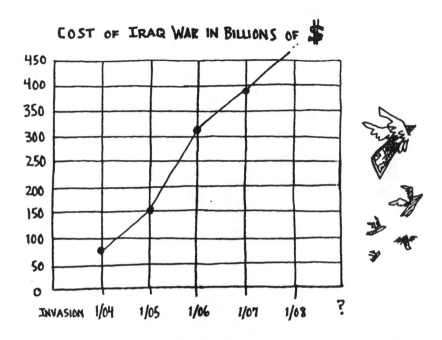

COST OF IRAQ WAR IN BILLIONS OF $

| | INVASION | 1/04 | 1/05 | 1/06 | 1/07 | 1/08 | ? |

He was unequivocal about Iraq: the U.S. should have all troops out of the country within 16 months. He said he would meet the President of neighboring Iran without preconditions— but refused to rule out the use of military force against it.

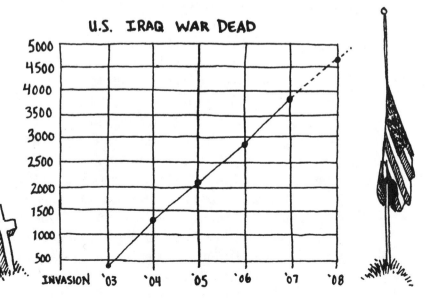

U.S. IRAQ WAR DEAD

| | INVASION | '03 | '04 | '05 | '06 | '07 | '08 |

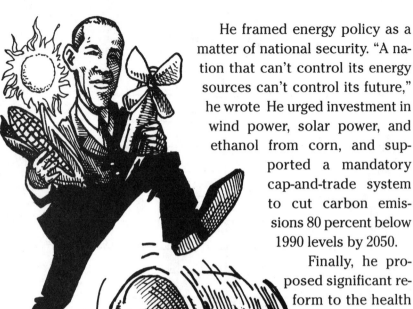

He framed energy policy as a matter of national security. "A nation that can't control its energy sources can't control its future," he wrote He urged investment in wind power, solar power, and ethanol from corn, and supported a mandatory cap-and-trade system to cut carbon emissions 80 percent below 1990 levels by 2050.

Finally, he proposed significant reform to the health care system: "We should be able to provide basic coverage to every single American," he wrote. "A basic, high-quality health-care plan," available to all, could be delivered through expansion of existing insurance pools, "like the one set up for federal employees," or by creating new pools. Private companies could compete to provide the plan. All records would be digital. Savings from new efficiencies, he projected, would allow immediate coverage for all uninsured children, and subsidies to insure low-income families.

Initial polls showed three leaders in the race for the Democratic nomination: New York Senator and former First Lady Hillary Clinton with about 35 percent of voters, Obama with around 25 percent, and former North Carolina Senator and 2004 vice presidential candidate John Edwards with 10-15 percent. The other candidates, New Mexico Governor Bill Richardson, Connecticut Senator Chris Dodd, Delaware Senator Joe Biden, Ohio Congressman Dennis Kucinich, and former Alaska Senator Mike Gravel, lagged far behind.

Behind the scenes, his staff used the Internet to build a nationwide volunteer organization, and fundraising juggernaut. The campaign website allowed individuals to stay informed about national and local efforts; make telephone calls to voters through a central database and update records based on results; and start mini-campaigns, complete with fundraising systems, blogs and events, to organize people in their geographic area or with shared interests. Managers guided the torrent of activism harnessed by the system first to one battleground, then another.

The public responded. On 16 January, a University of North Dakota graduate started "Barack Obama (One Million Strong for Barack)," on the Facebook social networking site. The group attracted over 100,000 members in nine days: one of the fastest growth rates ever seen at Facebook. There were more than 250,000 members when Obama officially launched his campaign on 11 February. The biggest pro-Clinton group on the site at the time had just 3,251 members. Chris Hughes, Facebook's co-founder, joined Obama's campaign that month. An "Obama application," that tied together these tens of thousands of supporters, soon appeared.

The impact of these grassroots efforts became clear on 31 March when fundraising reports for the first quarter were released. Obama was much closer to Clinton than the polls suggested. The New York senator had collected $26 million, Obama $25.6 million, and Edwards $12 million. The other candidates were literally out of the money. Crucially, although their gross totals were similar, the average size of Obama's donations was much smaller than those for Clinton. Obama, unlike Clinton, also refused to accept money from lobbyists. In sum, the Illinois senator had a much broader base of financial support.

Obama maintained his grip on the imagination of Internet users and younger voters throughout the summer and fall as the candidates criss-crossed the country to gain media attention, meet voters, and raise money. His youth, campaign themes, relative centrism, and opposition to the Iraq war were key selling points. In June, a YouTube video called "I Got a Crush on Obama" featuring a scantily dressed "Obama Girl" who crooned her affection for the senator and dismissed his rivals, became a hit. Several million people watched it. On 2 July, the campaign announced Obama had raised $32 million in the second quarter, far above the previous record for the period and more than Clinton's $27 million and Edwards' $9 million. Obama had 154,000 contributors, more than double the 60,000 who donated to Clinton. In December, there was a wave of publicity when billionaire Oprah Winfrey, host of the most popular television talk show in the country, endorsed him.

The Iowa caucuses, held 3 January 2008 constituted the first vote of the campaign. Party members assembled in 1,784 locations, one for each precinct, across the state. Arcane procedures governed the assemblies. Clinton was expected to do well because of her deep connections to party leaders—the result of eight years as first lady and seven as a senator. Some observers harbored concerns that an African-American candidate would have difficulty in a state that was 94.6 percent white. In the event, turnout shattered expectations—over 227,000 Democrats voted, compared to 122,193 in 2004—and Obama's careful organization brought victory: he won 38 percent of ballots, Edwards 30 percent, and Clinton 29 percent. The message was dramatic: Clinton's nomination was not a forgone conclusion. Obama was a contender.

Destiny was at hand, Obama said in his victory speech. "On this January night—at this defining moment in history—you have done what the cynics said we couldn't do. We are choosing hope over fear. We're choosing unity over division, and sending a powerful message that change is coming to America." He continued, "This was the moment when the improbable beat what Washington always said was inevitable. This was the moment when we tore down barriers that have divided us for too long—when we rallied people of all parties and ages to a common cause; when we finally gave Americans who'd never participated in politics a reason to stand up and to do so. This was the moment when we finally beat back the politics of fear, and doubt, and cynicism; the politics where we tear each other down instead of lifting this country up. This was the moment. Years from now, you'll look back and you'll say that this was the moment—this was the place—where America remembered what it means to hope."

The vote had an immediate impact. Senators Biden and Dodd withdrew from the race. Obama leapt to a 10-point lead in polls for the New Hampshire primary—an election, rather than a series of caucus meetings as in Iowa—scheduled for five days later.

A quartet of bleary candidates—Clinton, Edwards, Obama, and Richardson, the top four finishers in Iowa—gathered 48 hours later in Manchester, New Hampshire for an ABC News/Facebook debate. Edwards sided with Obama, and attacked Clinton as a standard-bearer for the status quo. "Every time he speaks out for change, every time I fight for change, the forces of status quo are going to attack—every single time," he said, referencing Obama by his side. The New York senator, playing to her theme of experience, appeared to accept his premise: "We don't need to be raising the false hopes of our country about what can be delivered," she said. A few days later, Clinton choked up in response to a woman who asked how she persevered despite the strain of the campaign . . . and who did her hair. It was not clear what caused the spark of emotion: the arduousness of the campaign, the reference to her appearance, which seemed to have little to do with qualification to be president, or some other reason. Regardless, the exchange created a surge of publicity for the senator. She defied expectations and narrowly won the primary with 39 percent of the vote, to 36 percent for Obama, 17 percent for Edwards, and about five percent for Richardson. The New Mexican, the first Hispanic candidate for President, withdrew from the race on 10 January. Clinton won in Michigan on 15 January with 55 percent of the vote, but the decision was largely ignored because the state had broken party rules by scheduling its vote when it did. It was unclear whether its delegates would be seated at the convention. Obama's name was not even on the ballot.

The next two contests were a caucus in Nevada and a primary in South Carolina. Clinton won the first, 51 percent to 45 percent, but Obama ran strongly across the state and ultimately won 13 delegates to her 12. Edwards, who had taken an increasingly uncompromising anti-business line in his speeches, gained less than five percent of the votes and captured no Nevada delegates. Kucinich, who had attracted only a tiny fraction of the electorate and had been largely ignored by the media, withdrew from the race on 24 January.

South Carolina, "Where the Confederate flag still flies," as Obama later said, was the first Southern state and the first with a large African-American population to hold a primary: just under one-third of its citizens are black. Obama carried it by 55 percent to Clinton's 27 percent—58 percent to her 23 percent among every age group except voters over 65. The race also revealed what appeared to be the organizational limits of the Clinton campaign, which had focused its resources on earlier states. "Obama's people had been organizing and cleaning lists since August, building an organization with real leadership and a genuine organizing base. . . . The Clinton campaign did not have anything close to that, having spent its time organizing in Iowa, New Hampshire and Nevada," wrote blogger Matt Stoller. When President Clinton compared Obama's win to that of earlier African-American presidential candidate Jesse Jackson—"Jesse Jackson won South Carolina in '84 and '88. Jackson ran a good campaign. And Obama ran a good campaign here," he said—blogs erupted in outrage at a perceived racially-charged slight to Obama's achievement.

Obama won significant endorsements after his South Carolina victory. Massachusetts Senator Ted Kennedy, his niece Caroline, daughter of President John F. Kennedy, and his son Patrick, a Rhode Island congressman, endorsed the "Kenyan Kennedy," as Obama's staff had called him in 2000, on 28 January. "I feel change in the air," Senator Kennedy said. Obama "offers that same sense of hope and inspiration" that her father did, Caroline said. On 1 February, the 3.2 million member online activist group MoveOn.org endorsed him, the first Democratic presidential primary endorsement in the organization's history. The group's members, who voted online, favored Obama over Clinton 70 percent to 30 percent. The New York senator carried Florida 50 percent to 33 for Obama at the end of January, but since, as with Michigan, the state had broken party rules by scheduling its vote too early, neither candidate campaigned there and it was not clear if its delegates would count. Edwards dropped out on 30 January.

The race was now between Obama and Clinton, but there was no clear leader. The fierce contest between two historic candidates riveted both domestic and international attention.

All eyes turned to 5 February, known as "Super Tuesday," because on that day voters in 22 states would assign 1,681 delegates. A total of 2,118 delegates was required for nomination. The result was inconclusive: Obama won more states, but Clinton carried the popular vote and gained three more delegates, 837 to 834. News broke the next day that suggested shakiness inside Clinton's campaign: she had been forced to loan her team $5 million at the end of January.

Then Obama began a winning streak that lasted more than a month, encompassed big and small states across the country, and left him with an advantage in delegates, popular perception, and the perception of the approximately 825 unelected "Superdelegate" party insiders, that would prove decisive. On 9 February, Obama won three states and a territory by huge margins: Louisiana 57-36, Nebraska 68-32, Washington 68-31, and the Virgin Islands 90-8. He won Maine 59-40 on 10 February, the District of Columbia 75-24, Virginia 64-35, and Maryland 61-36 two days later, and Wisconsin 58-41 and Hawaii 76-24 on 19 February. The victories confirmed what earlier results suggested: Obama's Internet-centered campaign, and his popular support, had both breadth and depth.

Attention focused on the new frontrunner, and a series of controversies rocked the campaign. On 19 February, Clinton's aides observed that portions of a speech Obama gave on 16 February were similar to an address his campaign co-chair Deval Patrick, the Governor of Massachusetts, had given in 2006. They suggested plagiarism. Obama dismissed the controversy with ease: he acknowledged Patrick's assistance; the Governor said he was flattered; and the public shrugged. A contretemps on 25 February over a 2006 photo of Obama wearing traditional Somali dress—which some tabloids and websites described as "Muslim" clothing—during a visit to Kenya after his election to the U.S. Senate, was equally swiftly dismissed. Senator Dodd, his former rival, endorsed Obama on 26 February.

By 4 March, when Clinton finally won Ohio, Texas and Rhode Island, analysts armed with sharp pencils had concluded that, barring a cataclysm, an Obama nomination was only a matter of time. John McCain clinched the Republican nomination the same evening.

The Clinton campaign waited to see if the trial of Chicago real estate developer Antoin "Tony" Rezko, which began on 6 March, might be cataclysmic for Obama. Rezko was charged with using his clout as an adviser to the Illinois governor to extort money from firms that did business with the state. There was no direct connection between Obama and the charges—but the presidential candidate had a long history with the defendant. Rezko had offered Obama a job when Obama became president of the Harvard Law Review, but the student turned him down. Later, Rezko was a client of Obama's law firm Davis, Miner, and Obama spent five hours on matters related to a partnership between a church group and Rezmar Corp., Rezko's firm, to build low-income housing. In 1997, Allison Davis, a partner at the firm, left and partnered with Rezko to form the New Kenwood real estate company. Obama, then a state senator, wrote letters to state and federal officials to urge them to approve a housing development for low-income senior citizens proposed by the company. "It was going to help people in his district," his campaign said in 2007. Finally, Rezko donated numerous times to Obama's campaigns, although not to his presidential bid, and was a member of the finance committee for his U.S. Senate campaign. Total donations from Rezko, his family members, and his associates, to the 2004 campaign totaled about $250,000.

ANTOIN REZKO

This was the context when, on 15 June 2005, Obama and his wife bought a house for $1.65 million (financed largely by earnings from his books)—and Rezko's wife bought an adjoining vacant lot on the same day from the same seller for $625,000. The Obamas paid $300,000 below the asking price for the house. Rezko's wife purchased her lot for the asking price. The seller, a doctor, later said the Obamas had made two earlier bids for the house that were even lower, and that the price he accepted was the best he could get. In February 2006, the Obamas bought one-sixth of the lot, a 10-foot strip that ran next to their property, from Rezko's wife for $104,000—one-sixth of the purchase price—to expand their garden. Details of these transactions came to light in November, after Rezko's October indictment. Obama, in response to questions from the press, termed the transactions related to his house "boneheaded." "It was a mistake to have been engaged with him at all in this or any other personal business dealing that would allow him, or anyone else, to believe that he had done me a favor," he said.

Obama had not, however, done anything illegal. The issue faded. In March 2008, his 2010 U.S. Senate re-election campaign committee announced it would give the contributions by Rezko and his family members and associates to charity. In June, the developer was convicted on 16 counts of corruption and went to prison.

The second week of March 2008 brought a new crisis. ABC News announced on 13 March that it had reviewed videotapes sold in the lobby of Trinity Church and found they showed repeated denunciations of the United States by Reverend Wright. "The government gives them the drugs, builds bigger prisons, passes a three-strike law and then wants us to sing 'God Bless America.' No, no, no, God damn America, that's in the Bible for killing innocent people," he said in a 2003 sermon. The U.S., he said, should not have been surprised by the 9/11 attacks. "We bombed Nagasaki, and we nuked far more than the thousands in New York and the Pentagon, and we never batted an eye," he preached on 16 September 2001. Indeed, the former marine said, "We have supported state terrorism against the Palestinians and black South Africans, and now we are indignant because the stuff we have done overseas is now brought right back to our own front yards. America's chickens are coming home to roost." Obama said he was not present when Wright gave the sermons at issue.

The uproar that resulted dominated campaign coverage for days and might have derailed Obama's campaign because it cut to core issues of race, national identity, and politics.

Instead, the candidate took advantage of the attention and spoke directly to these issues in an address titled "A More Perfect Union" that he delivered at the National Constitution Center in Philadelphia on 18 March. Wright's statements showed "a profoundly distorted view of this country," he said. Yet the former marine was also "a man who spoke to me about our obligations to love one another; to care for the sick and lift up the poor," Obama said. "I can no more disown him than I can my white grandmother—a woman who helped raise me, a woman who sacrificed again and again for me, a woman who loves me as much as she loves anything in this world, but a woman who once confessed her fear of black men who passed by her on the street, and who on more than one occasion has uttered racial or ethnic stereotypes that made me cringe," he added. "The profound mistake of Reverend Wright's sermons is not that he spoke about racism in our society. It's that he spoke as if our society was static; as if no progress has been made. But what we know—what we have seen—is that America can change."

Finally, he said, "We have a choice in this country. We can accept a politics that breeds division, and conflict, and cynicism. . . . We can play Reverend Wright's sermons on every channel, every day and talk about them from now until the election, and make the only question in this campaign whether or not the American people think that I somehow believe or sympathize with his most offensive words. . . . Or, at this moment, in this election, we can come together and say, 'Not this time.' This time we want to talk about the crumbling schools that are stealing the future of black children and white children and Asian children and Hispanic children and Native American children. This time we want to reject the cynicism that tells us that these kids can't learn; that those kids who don't look like us are somebody else's problem. The children of America are not those kids, they are our kids, and we will not let them fall behind in a 21st century economy. Not this time." The speech received a favorable reaction, and the storm abated.

11 April produced "Bittergate." The HuffingtonPost.com website posted an explanation Obama gave at a private fundraiser in San Francisco of the challenges he faced with working-class voters in Pennsylvania and Indiana. "It's not surprising they get bitter," he said, referring to decades of constrained economic opportunities. "They cling to guns or religion or antipathy to people who aren't like them or anti-immigrant sentiment or anti-trade sentiment as a way to explain their frustrations." Clinton said the remarks were "not reflective of the values and beliefs of Americans." McCain said Obama showed "breathtaking" elitism. Obama challenged the accusations, and noted in response to the charge of elitism that he had been raised by a single mother who relied for a time on food stamps, but conceded he could have been more diplomatic.

The first meeting between the candidates in seven weeks took place on 16 April in Philadelphia, six days before the Pennsylvania primary, at a debate hosted by ABC News. Expectations for a substantive exchange were high. Instead, the hosts focused on superficialities such as whether the candidates would choose each other for vice president (they declined to say), how often Obama wore an American flag lapel pin (occasionally), and how well he knew Bill Ayers, a professor of education at the University of Illinois at Chicago. Ayers, now a "valued member of the Chicago community," according to its mayor Richard M. Daley, was a leader of the Weather Underground in the 1960s. The group declared war against the United States and took credit for bombing two dozen public buildings, including the Pentagon. It fell apart after a 1970 explosion destroyed a Greenwich Village townhouse where members were building a nail bomb, apparently to attack an officer's dance at Fort Dix in New Jersey; three were killed. Ayers subsequently spent a decade on the run until charges against him were dropped because of prosecutorial misconduct. In 1995, he organized an event at his Hyde Park home to introduce Obama to neighbors and friends, and donated $200 to Obama's state senate campaign. "The notion that somehow as a consequence of me knowing somebody who engaged in detestable acts 40 years ago, when I was eight years old, somehow reflects on me and my values, doesn't make much sense," Obama responded. "This kind of game, in which anybody who I know, regardless of how flimsy the relationship is, is somehow—somehow their ideas could be attributed to me—I think the American people are smarter than that," he added.

Clinton needed to win Pennsylvania by 20 percent or more to give her a realistic chance to catch Obama, given the relatively small number of primaries that remained. She won by ten percent. A sense of inevitability grew around Obama's campaign.

The Wright storm flared anew on 28 April. The reverend did not follow the candidate's conciliatory lead in his Philadelphia address. Instead, in a speech to the National Press Club in Washington, D.C., he called his congregant insincere: "Politicians say what they say and do what they do because of electability," Wright said: "He had to distance himself because he's a politician." The pastor repeated his assertions that the U.S. government may have introduced the AIDS virus into the African-American community, and that the country might in part be responsible for the 9/11 attacks. Obama broke with his pastor the next day. He decried the address as "a bunch of rants that aren't grounded in the truth."

NATIONAL PRESS CLUB

Victory in North Carolina and the failure by Clinton to do better than a virtual tie in Indiana on 6 May made Obama's nomination all but certain. The New York senator declined to concede, however, and the contest continued.

Trinity Church was back in the news on 25 May: a story that seemingly would not die. Michael Pfleger, the white pastor of a neighboring Chicago church and long-time acquaintance of Obama, mocked Senator Clinton from the Trinity pulpit during a guest sermon. "I really believe that she just always thought, 'This is mine. I'm Bill's wife, I'm white and this is mine. I just gotta get up and step into the plate.' And then out of nowhere came, 'Hey, I'm Barack Obama.' And she said, 'Oh, damn, where did you come from? I'm white. I'm entitled. There's a black man stealing my show.'" Obama resigned from the church, his spiritual home for two decades, a few days later. "We don't want to have to answer for everything that's stated in the church," he said.

MICHAEL PFLEGER

The last hope for Clinton faded on 1 June when the Democratic Party's Rules Committee decided that delegates elected in Michigan and Florida would be seated—but would receive only one-half votes as punishment for scheduling their primaries earlier than allowed by party rules. Obama was awarded all uncommitted Michigan delegates. His campaign had urged supporters to vote "uncommitted" since his name did not appear on the ballot. The 15-12 vote left Obama's delegate lead intact: 202 before the Rules Committee vote and 174 afterwards. Even if all the delegates had been granted a full vote, Obama still would have had more delegates than Clinton.

PRIMARIES IN DISPUTE

In what he said was, "a defining moment for our nation," Obama announced after polls closed on 3 June in South Dakota and Montana, the last two primary states, that he would be the Democratic nominee. He spoke to the nation from the St. Paul arena where the Republicans planned to hold their convention in September. The next day, he ordered the Democratic Party to stop taking money from lobbyists. On 7 June, Clinton conceded and endorsed Obama. "I ask all of you to join me in working as hard for Barack Obama as you have for me," she said to her supporters.

To underscore the point, the two appeared together at the end of June in Unity, a tiny town in south-central New Hampshire where each received 107 votes in the primary.

Obama's primary campaign had raised over $295 million from approximately 1.5 million individuals. It was an unprecedented achievement, impossible before the Internet. Given the magnitude of this sum and predictions he could raise more from millions of fresh donors, Obama decided to reject $84 million in public funding for the general election. If he had accepted it, he would have been barred from accepting contributions from individuals. "The public financing of presidential elections as it exists today is broken, and we face opponents who have become masters at gaming this broken system," he said in a statement. He was the first major party presidential candidate since Watergate to decline public funds. In *The Audacity of Hope*, he wrote, "Public financing of campaigns or free television and radio time could drastically reduce the constant scrounging for money and the influence of special interests." Now, he showed his practical side.

The pressure of the soaring ambitions Obama had unleashed for some in his campaign began to build. In an informal talk with his Chicago campaign staff in mid-June, he said, "We don't have an option now. When we were at the beginning of this thing in Iowa, if I lost Iowa, it would have been okay, you know? One of the other Democrats would have emerged and they would have carried the banner and we would have joined their campaign and we would have moved forward and the country would move in a better direction. But because we won, we now have no choice." We don't have a choice, he continued, "because now if we screw this up, all those people that I've met, who really need help, they're not going to get help. Those of you that are concerned about global warming, I don't care what John McCain says, he is not going to push that agenda. All those who are concerned about Darfur, I guarantee you they are not going to spend any political capital on that. Those of you who are concerned about education, there will be a bunch of lip service and then there will be more of the same. Those of you who are concerned about making sure that there's a sense of fairness in our economy, it will be less fair. So now everybody is counting on you, not just me, and I know that's a heavy weight but also what a magnificent position to find yourselves in, where the whole country is counting on you to change it for the better. Now those moments don't come around very often. And here you are, five months away from having transformed the country and made history and changed the world. So we've got to seize it, so rest up a little bit, but come back, ready to go . . . and fired up. I love you guys, let's go win the election."

6/11/08 –
6/25/08

After a remarkable journey from Hawaii to Harvard, the poorest neighborhoods of Chicago to the halls of power, the classroom to the podium of national discourse—and from a wandering childhood to a rooted home—Obama is modest about his achievements. Of comparisons to Martin Luther King, Jr. he has said, "He spoke poetry and I am prose." More generally, he told an interviewer, "I'm constantly reminding myself that a lot of these opportunities that have opened up for me are beyond my control." Whatever the balance between fate and self-determination, Obama has accomplished much with the opportunities that have been under his control.

FURTHER READING

BarackObamaForBeginners.com is the best place to begin for additional information. The site contains an updated list of print and online resources, including links to numerous relevant video clips, a timeline, and a complete list of sources for this book.

The best biography of Obama is *Obama: From Promise to Power* by *Chicago Tribune* reporter David Mendell. The book, published in 2007, provides a comprehensive review of Obama's early history, and a wealth of detail about his political career from the Illinois Senate through his decision to run for President.

Obama has written two books. *Dreams from My Father: A Story of Race and Inheritance,* published in 1995 and reissued in 2004, is a memoir that describes his childhood in Indonesia and Hawaii, college years in Los Angeles and New York, work as a community organizer in Chicago, and trip to Kenya in 1988 to meet some of his relatives. The book offers numerous insights into the politician's history and the evolution of his thoughts on such issues as race, poverty, politics, religion, and his family.

The Audacity of Hope: Thoughts on Reclaiming the American Dream, his second book, written during his first year as U.S. Senator, was published in 2006. The volume has sections that are reminiscent of the intimacy that characterizes *Dreams from My Father* but is in general more formal. Obama describes his thoughts about the current political divisions in the country; tells the story of his campaign for the U.S. Senate; outlines his positions on such issues as the economy, health, energy policy, race, faith, and constitutional jurisprudence; and concludes, as in his first book, with observations about his family. Obama won the 2006 and 2008 Grammy Awards for Best Spoken Word Album for the audiobook editions of *Dreams from My Father* and *The Audacity of Hope* respectively.

There are numerous other volumes about Obama—and likely to be still more in the future. Titles with specialized appeal include *Obamamania! The English Language, Barackafied,* a lexicon by the editors of Slate.com, and *Yes We Can! A Biography of Barack Obama,* a children's book intended for reading levels 9 through 12 by Garen Thomas.

The Internet is an excellent source of information about Obama. Websites that are particularly useful include the following. Direct links to all of these are available at BarackObamaForBeginners.com.

- BarackObama.com. The candidate's website contains transcripts of all of his major recent speeches, videos of Obama, recent news, and basic biographical information. It allows first-person interaction with the online campaign tools described in this book.
- Wikipedia @ Wikipedia.org/wiki/Barack_Obama. The online encyclopedia has detailed pages of comprehensively-sourced biographical information, and additional pages on key elements of this book, from Obama's father and mother to political events.
- *Chicago Tribune* @ ChicagoTribune.com/news/politics/obama. The newspaper has an extensive biographical profile of Obama, an "Obama blog," an "Obama tracker" that shows his recent movements, a photographic tour of locations important to Obama's life in Chicago, and even a Quiz to test your knowledge about Obama.
- *Chicago Sun-Times* @ SunTimes.com/news/politics/obama/index.html. The journal's "Barack Obama" center offers a constantly updated index of news related to Obama, access to its deep archive of stories about the politician, and photo galleries.
- *New York Times* @ Politics.NYTimes.com/Election-Guide/2008/index.html. The best single online reference for news reports, statistics, and interactive maps related to recent U.S. political history.
- *The New Yorker* @ NewYorker.com. A pair of profiles of Obama and one of his wife Michelle are available online. "The Candidate: How the son of a Kenyan economist became an Illinois Everyman," by William Finnegan was published on 31 May 2004. "The Conciliator: Where is Barack Obama coming from?" by Larissa MacFarquhar appeared on 7 May 2007. "The Other Obama: Michelle Obama and the politics of candor," by Lauren Collins was released 10 March 2008. Search for the pieces by title or author.

ACKNOWLEDGMENTS

My first acknowledgment is to my wife Xuan. Every word in this book is supported by her love and encouragement. The good cheer of my son Marco buoyed my spirits. Macallan K. Nein kept me grounded.

Dr. Robert Neer, my father, and Ann Eldridge, my stepmother, provided spot-on editing advice. My brother, professor Richard Neer, helped clarify important details. My sister-in-law Erika Dudley, and nephew Teddy "T-Rex" Neer, offered encouragement.

A book is a team in print. Chip Fleischer is our leader: he brought concision and clarity. He has been my friend for 25 years, and I am proud now to add collaborator to the ties that bind us. Dawn Reshen-Doty conceived of this volume: it would not exist without her. The careful attentions of Merrilee Warholak and Helga Schmidt helped make this tome a reality; Christa Demment González and Doran Dal Pra helped make the world aware of it.

Since a picture is worth 1,000 words Joe Lee, our Illustrator, has contributed far more than I. The dramatic cover and careful typesetting are the work of David Janik.

Ester Murdukhayeva, our researcher, was my back-stop. She studies legal and criminal history at Columbia College and plans to begin law school next year.

David Kravitz, who read part of the manuscript, and Charley Blandy (my co-Editors at BlueMassGroup.com), Steve Swartzman and Maureen Marzano deserve special thanks.

The last, not least, acknowledgment is to my mother, who continues to infuse my world with dreams, and the discipline of aspiration. I hope this little book would please her.

About the Author:

Bob Neer is writing his dissertation to complete his J.D.-Ph.D. degree in U.S. History at Columbia University. He received his M. Phil. in U.S. History from Columbia in 2007, and a J.D. and an M.A. in U.S. History, both from Columbia, in 1991. He studied Southeast Asian politics as a Fulbright Scholar at the National University of Singapore and is a *magna cum laude* graduate of Harvard College. He is a Co-Founder and Editor of BlueMassGroup.com, the most widely read political blog in New England. He lives in New York City with his wife, son and border collie.

About the Illustrator:

Joe Lee is an illustrator, cartoonist, writer and clown. A graduate of Ringling Brothers, Barnum and Bailey's Clown College, he worked for many years as a circus clown. He is also the illustrator for many other For Beginners books including: *Dada and Surrealism For Beginners*, *Postmodernism For Beginners*, and *Shakespeare For Beginners*. Joe lives with his wife, Mary Bess, three cats, and two dogs (Toby and Jack).

THE FOR BEGINNERS® SERIES

AFRICAN HISTORY FOR BEGINNERS:	ISBN 978-1-934389-18-8
ANARCHISM FOR BEGINNERS:	ISBN 978-1-934389-32-4
ARABS & ISRAEL FOR BEGINNERS:	ISBN 978-1-934389-16-4
ASTRONOMY FOR BEGINNERS:	ISBN 978-1-934389-25-6
BLACK HISTORY FOR BEGINNERS:	ISBN 978-1-934389-19-5
THE BLACK HOLOCAUST FOR BEGINNERS:	ISBN 978-1-934389-03-4
BLACK WOMEN FOR BEGINNERS:	ISBN 978-1-934389-20-1
CHOMSKY FOR BEGINNERS:	ISBN 978-1-934389-17-1
DADA & SURREALISM FOR BEGINNERS:	ISBN 978-1-934389-00-3
DECONSTRUCTION FOR BEGINNERS:	ISBN 978-1-934389-26-3
DERRIDA FOR BEGINNERS:	ISBN 978-1-934389-11-9
EASTERN PHILOSOPHY FOR BEGINNERS:	ISBN 978-1-934389-07-2
EXISTENTIALISM FOR BEGINNERS:	ISBN 978-1-934389-21-8
FOUCAULT FOR BEGINNERS:	ISBN 978-1-934389-12-6
HEIDEGGER FOR BEGINNERS:	ISBN 978-1-934389-13-3
ISLAM FOR BEGINNERS:	ISBN 978-1-934389-01-0
KIERKEGAARD FOR BEGINNERS:	ISBN 978-1-934389-14-0
LINGUISTICS FOR BEGINNERS:	ISBN 978-1-934389-28-7
MALCOLM X FOR BEGINNERS:	ISBN 978-1-934389-04-1
NIETZSCHE FOR BEGINNERS:	ISBN 978-1-934389-05-8
THE OLYMPICS FOR BEGINNERS:	ISBN 978-1-934389-33-1
PHILOSOPHY FOR BEGINNERS:	ISBN 978-1-934389-02-7
PLATO FOR BEGINNERS:	ISBN 978-1-934389-08-9
POSTERMODERNISM FOR BEGINNERS:	ISBN 978-1-934389-09-6
SARTRE FOR BEGINNERS:	ISBN 978-1-934389-15-7
SHAKESPEARE FOR BEGINNERS:	ISBN 978-1-934389-29-4
STRUCTURALISM & POSTRUCTURALISM FOR BEGINNERS:	ISBN 978-1-934389-10-2
ZEN FOR BEGINNERS:	ISBN 978-1-934389-06-5

www.forbeginnersbooks.com